SMASH & CARVE
Golf

The Art of Ball Striking

WITH SCOTT MINNI
scgolf@axion.net

www.smashandcarvegolf.com

Canadian Cataloguing in Publication Data
Minni, Scott
Smash & Carve Golf

ISBN 0-9685155-0-9

1. Golf. I. Title 796.352 3 C99-910379-2
GV965.M55 1999

third edition

Creative & Photography by One Designs

Printed in Vancouver, BC Canada
Good Impressions Printing Ltd.

A Tribute to Ben Hogan
1912 ~ 1997

"I feel sorry for rich kids now. I really do. Because they`re never going to have the opportunity I had. Because I knew tough things. And I had a tough day all my life and I can handle tough things. They can`t. And every day that I progressed was a joy to me and I recognized it every day. I don`t think I could have done what I`ve done if I hadn`t had the tough days to begin with."

Ben Hogan

In his day Ben Hogan was dealt some pretty difficult cards. Through hard work and nothing else he rose to the top to become one of the greatest golf legends of all time. I was never fortunate enough to meet Mr. Hogan personally but through various books, interviews, and the documentary video, I came to learn that Hogan started in poverty and overcame unbelievable obstacles to reach his goals. It`s such a shame that major golf events were not televised until 1954 at the U.S. Open, the year after Hogan had his incredible Triple Slam in 1953. He won all three majors he played in; The Masters, The U.S. Open, and, on his only visit overseas, the British Open. The PGA Championship was to be the fourth major that year, but seeing as how it overlapped with the British Open winning the Grand Slam was not possible.

I write this tribute not only to recognize Hogan's climb to golfing greatness but also to acknowledge his continuous uphill climb from setbacks and bad breaks. This man had good reason to quit many times over. In February, 1949, while driving home from Phoenix, Arizona to Fort Worth, Texas after a tour event, he and his wife Valerie were met head on by a thirty-seven passenger bus on a foggy Texas highway. Upon impact, Hogan dove across his wife`s lap to avoid some of the 20,000 pounds hurtling towards him. Unfortunately, his legs were trapped on the driver's side and were so severely damaged he lived in pain, and with a limp, for the rest of his life. After the historic accident, Hogan was not capable of playing in his regular thirty tournaments per year; instead he played in only five or six. For the rest of Hogan's career, his roster for the golf season would consist of only the Masters, the U.S. Open, Fort Worth's Colonial, the Seminole Amateur-Professional and one or two others. After the accident, Hogan would never again play in the P.G.A. Championship because of its 36-hole match play format. This tournament would be impossible for his battered legs to handle, and the British Open was a one-shot deal in 1953.

Every tournament he played in after the accident would have been excruciating for his battered legs, since the last two rounds were always played on a Saturday; there was no Sunday golf unless a playoff was required! Hogan's courage was clearly demonstrated at the 1950 U.S. Open, just sixteen months after he had nearly been killed. During the third round, at about noon on Saturday, Hogan was nearly leveled by unbearable cramps in his tensor-bandaged legs. "That`s it. I just can`t make it," he said through clenched teeth to his caddie. "No Mr. Hogan, you can`t quit," the boy had supposedly said, "because I don`t work for quitters." After this Hogan found the strength to carry on and amazingly won the tournament in an eighteen hole playoff. It didn't end after 36 holes on Saturday—he had to play another round to really earn it, testing his will to the fullest again!

From what I have come to understand of Ben Hogan, his life had more than its share of disappointment and nothing ever came easy. The accident was one more survival test, a brush with death to add to his already hardened skin as this wasn't his first experience with tragedy. When he was just nine years old his father committed suicide in their home with a gun, and Bennie was in the house. From the age of ten until the age of twenty eight, for almost eighteen years after his father's death, Hogan lived in poverty.

He turned pro in 1930, at just eighteen. The first ten years of his professional career were disappointing to say the least, he barely made a cheque, yet he kept practicing more than anyone had ever seen. But all the practice wasn`t paying off in those early years, so what could have kept him going? "I just loved to practice," he would say later.

Byron Nelson was a long time friend of Hogan's, going back as far as the 1927 Glen Garden Caddie Tournament, when they were both fifteen. Nelson matured early at golf and enjoyed his most productive years before the age of thirty-four. He retired from full-time play in 1946, the same year Hogan would win his first major. Hogan had to watch his friend Byron enjoy early success at golf, along with financial rewards, while he struggled to scratch out a living. The breakthrough year for Ben Hogan was 1940 when he won his first individual tournament and became the leading money winner. Finally, he was on his way. Again in 1942 he was the leading money winner before the season was stopped halfway through due to the war. This same year the U.S. Open was renamed the Hail America Open and Hogan won the event on the strength of a second round 62. The tournament should have been Hogan's first major. Unfortunately the Hail America was never counted as a major, even though the tournament was identical to a U.S. Open with a winning medal the same as the other four medals he won. Just when life was getting good, setbacks would once again test his spirit. The next year's golf season was canceled due to the war, and Hogan was drafted on March 1, 1943. He would not compete in another major until the 1946 Masters.

Hogan's best years were shortened when you count the three and a half years he lost during the war and the one year he lost due to his accident. Compared to his friend Byron Nelson who was an early bloomer with a real lucky streak, Ben Hogan lost four and a half productive years in his prime; not very encouraging for an already late bloomer. Lucky Byron didn`t get drafted, due to a medical reason, and as a result, he enjoyed his historic year of 1945 by winning eighteen times, with eleven in a row, setting a record that will never be broken. Fortunately for Nelson, most of the competitive field, including Hogan, was still in the service for most of that year and there really wasn`t much challenge for Nelson. When Hogan got out of the service in August, 1945, one of the first tournaments he played was the Portland Open. Before the tournament Nelson had acquired the nickname 'Mr. Golf', but Hogan won the tournament, shooting the lowest seventy-two-hole score in tour history with a 261. His rounds of 65-69-63-64 were two below Nelson`s old mark. Jimmy Demaret shook his hand saying, "Congratulations Ben!" To which Hogan flatly remarked "I guess that takes care of this 'Mr. Golf' business."

Hogan achieved his greatness through constant study and practice. "He dug it out of the ground", said Jules Alexander. He prepared for the 1953 Masters at Seminole in Florida with an exhaustive and diligent practice schedule. Six hundred balls before lunch, fifty with each of twelve clubs at three balls per minute, a snack and some rest, and then a repeat of the whole routine in the afternoon. Hogan invented practice. I once heard that he hit balls until his hands would bleed. Others used to laugh at him for practicing because he always outworked everybody. He was the sole judge of his standards and there wasn`t enough daylight in any one day to practice all the shots required for golf. He once stated that every day of practice missed would take him one day longer to be good, and that the more he practiced 'the luckier he got'!

The intensity with which Hogan lived and worked gave rise to these famous quotes, and they have served as motivational tools for many of the world`s best golfers over the years. But for all the truth and insight Hogan shared with us on the game, he was perhaps the only man in sports history to have discovered for himself a secret!

THE HOGAN SECRET was unique in the sports world. Where most games relied upon fundamentals and raw skill, golf had a 'Secret' supposedly only known to Hogan. For much of his early career his game was haunted by a nasty hook that kept him up at nights yelling, "Fore left". His Secret to golf ball control was initially introduced to him in March, 1940, by Henry Picard, a respected club pro and tour player who believed in Hogan. On the practice tee after a defeat in the Miami-Biltmore Four Ball Hogan had told Picard, "You told me I was going to be a great player, but I hook too much." Without directly asking for help, Picard knew that Hogan wanted his advice. Instructing Hogan to get his 5-iron, he said 5 minutes together was all they needed. This might have been the first formal lesson Hogan ever took; and the last. In that 5 minutes, Picard simply told Hogan to slice; to turn the left hand weak, aim left and shoot. Interestingly within two weeks after the tip from Picard, Hogan went on a hot streak and won his first individual event, The North and South Golf Championship followed that up with two more consecutive victories. Three wins in a row! Now he believed he could win!

After the early success, Picard's advice gradually wore off and Hogan was back to hooking everything by the time he was drafted into the army in 1942. Perhaps while in the Army Hogan really started to understand the full potential of the Picard tip; maybe even adding to it? Whatever he devised during the war certainly must have worked, because when he was discharged in August 1945, he was unstoppable. For the next three and a half years, until the accident in 1949 he won thirty-seven times, including three majors.Throughout the hot streak Hogan began to command attention with his golf game. The media and fellow touring professionals kept asking him, "What`s your secret?" "Not telling," he would reply. Hogan refused to comment on his secret, except to confirm that it did indeed exist. Almost ten years to the day of his discharge (from August 1945 to August 1955) he kept everybody guessing. One fellow competitor said, "He just looks like he knows more than the rest of us!" He finally revealed his Secret in the 1955 August 8 issue of Life Magazine, not surprisingly to widespread disappointment. The Secret simply involved 'anti-hook' swing maneuvers; essentially slicing and fading the ball at will! The public hated it. "What`s the fuss," they said, "I already know how to slice!" Basically, his plan was to 'eliminate the left side of the course' using three different swing fundamentals. They were: 1. The weak left hand grip: rotating the left hand to the left, showing maybe one knuckle when looking down at it; 2. Pronation: while taking the club back he fanned the blade of the club 'open'; 3. Cupping the left wrist inward at the top of the swing and coordinating this move with pronation on the take-away. These three moves when combined together make it virtually impossible to hit a hook. How ironic that more than ninety percent of all golfers already own these swing fundamentals. Anyone can slice, and Hogan acknowledged this when he said, "I doubt if it will be worth a doggone to the weekend duffer, and it will ruin a bad golfer." It`s probably why he didn`t include the information in his classic instructional book, 'Five Lessons-The Modern Fundamentals of Golf', published in 1957. The best players thought it was brilliant but they were a small percentage. There was no way he was going to include anything regarding the Secret in an instructional book because he knew what the public needed. Commenting on this he stated, "It probably won`t be of much help to anyone but the expert player, since most golfers are slicers, and to be an accomplished fader of the ball, one must first know how to draw it." This statement alone is the reason why he only shows 'right to left' mechanics in his text, such as a 'three knuckle, left hand grip' and 'hit from the inside'. While he never actually mentions ball flight, these fundamentals are just that, right to left.

Hogan was the perfect person to write an instructional book because he figured it all out for himself. He also had a little help along the way, not only from Henry Picard and his advise to slice, but from the lessons he used to teach. He once said, "I think I was a pretty fair teacher, providing the pupil was seriously interested in improving his game. Quite early in my career when I was serving as the professional at the Century Country Club in Purchase, N.Y., I did a great deal of teaching." As with any instructor today, Hogan probably taught a lot of slicers. Perhaps he combined this teaching experience with the tip from Picard and realized the potential benefits of the slice-swing action.

It had always amazed me that by following the fundamentals he taught in his book Five Lessons, one might be inclined to develop a nasty hook. It would seem then that Hogan`s Secret, essentially a slice-swing-action, might well have been included to balance those who had followed his text to the letter. They say he didn`t include these slice maneuvers in his instructional text. Now perhaps knowing the general golfing public, Hogan felt it best to leave this information out, because most golfers slice. But amazingly enough I have found some very interesting examples illustrating 'a leg' of his Secret in detail throughout the 'Five Lessons' (he just couldn`t resist!). For those of you that don`t own a copy of this classic book I suggest you get one as soon as possible — those that do please refer to page 51. Notice how the arrow is saying to 'point or flex the right elbow directly to the right hip'; compared to his left elbow they both look quite even, right?! Now please turn the page to 53 and tell me if this right arm position resembles anything even close to that on page 51? His right arm is much higher on page 53, showing a very 'open' shoulder alignment relative to his feet! An experienced golfer will know the difference between these two opposites. Right elbow down is more of a draw position and 'open' shoulders is a slice position. Perhaps he couldn`t resist and slipped in part of the Secret after all? Now, I know what you are thinking — you`re saying that they`re only sketches, right? There`s room for error, right? Not a chance. Hogan was a perfectionist. He would have examined this book thoroughly just like he did when the first run of Hogan golf clubs came down the line in the summer of `54. He inspected the gleaming new irons, hated them and gave instructions to "Scrap 'em". His partner was shocked over the prospect of losing a hundred-thousand dollars worth of product! That was a small fortune in those days but it didn`t matter, quality was everything, as it was with everything Hogan did. Page 78 shows another 'open' shoulder position with 'closed' feet (not even close to square), and the most blatant of all, the two facing pages 118 & 119. It couldn't be much more obvious than that. The beautifully crafted illustrations in the book were the work of Anthony Ravielli, a medical illustrator known for his precise drawing techniques. He could have, and would have changed a drawing at any time, even in a matter of minutes — which makes the opposite positions even more interesting. There was no fluke or oversight; the positions in the drawings were intentional!

Ben Hogan will always serve as an inspiration for many fine players and teachers alike. He was a truly amazing player and instructor, leaving behind a legacy and mystique that has never been surpassed. Hogan's story has achieved legendary status and is still one of the most talked about in the history of golf. Yet in learning more about Mr. Hogan, we discover that his legacy was not that mysterious after all. He took sheer will and determination and his passion for golf, and dedicated his life to teaching himself and others how to play their best. Through unbelievably tough work ethics Ben Hogan figured out for himself a way to achieve his goals both in life and golf, and leaves us with the knowledge and inspiration to do the same.

HOW TO APPROACH A LESSON

LESSON 1 BUILDING A SWING

LESSON 2 CONTACT

LESSON 3 DIRECTION

LESSON 4 SUPINATION

PRACTICE WITH A PURPOSE

How To Approach a Lesson

Let's get one thing straight before starting — Golf is not a natural game and there are no natural golfers! Now, it is true that some individuals are more athletic than others but learning golf is not unlike any other sport or activity you take an interest in; your progress will depend on how much attention you decide to give it. I find it a little amusing when I hear someone say, "does she ever make it look easy, what a natural." It makes me think that the admirer has no idea as to the time that person spent developing their talent. So it is with golf. To learn it you have to earn it!

All of us golfers share one thing in common, we all started as rookies. I always like to compare learning golf to learning how to play the piano — sure, anyone can play the piano, with two fingers, but how about getting all ten fingers in motion and playing a real piece? This is an acquired skill. Almost always, the admired talent has given their sport or activity plenty of time somewhere in their life, usually during a person's youth (before 18) when responsibilities are minimal. Remember those days; no job, no girlfriend, no husband — just school? This is the most productive learning time for anything, including golf, mainly because there are not a lot of responsibilities getting in the way. Your interest can be number one! Children are not more talented than adults, they just have more time for practice — and practice is the key to golf!

Someone once said, "golf cannot be taught, it must be learned." That is, if you are serious about improving rapidly, you will naturally be keen to research the game first on your own. You will fast realize that golf is not just a game, it is a lifestyle and is able to provide you with great information, from talking and sharing with other keen players, to watching videos, taking vacations and reading books. This background information will serve as a great foundation as you are learning the mechanics, and will eventually become a part of your game. The more prepared you are before you get to the lesson tee, the greater improvement will be seen.

I have been teaching golf now since 1985 and I have never wished I was in a different line of work. It can, at times, be a little demanding, usually because of a student's lack of enthusiasm towards understanding the theory, and not because of their actual physical performance. I have often wondered if starting my lessons in a classroom setting and initially taking a more theoretical approach would be more beneficial than starting on the range. A new student that is able to communicate with the teacher in the same language will have done some preparation before the lesson and will therefore derive the greatest benefits from it. Reading this text is a great start, for it will prepare you with the phrases and concepts that are common to golfers. Establishing a golf vocabulary early will speed your progress considerably.

Expect awkwardness, because it may not feel right to you when first introduced. That`s why it will be a good idea to practice some movements at home, and then have a qualified teaching pro help you to solidify the theory and develop the positions in a formal lesson. Experienced players are often asked to exaggerate a movement or position as part of their development. The exaggerating technique will help you to develop at a much faster rate. In fact I strongly encourage this method of instruction, since changing muscle memory makes an inch feel like a mile.

Smash & Carve is an instructional book divided into three categories: 1. Building a swing; 2. Contact; 3. Direction. These three categories, I feel, directly relate to anyone who plays golf. If you are a beginner, 'Lesson One, Building A Swing', will be your starting point, and the following lessons should be read in order. If you are past the beginner stage and have been working on your swing for a while, I want you to ask yourself this question: "do I need help with my *contact* or *direction*?" I guarantee it will be one or the other, if not both. Before coming to a lesson, it would be extremely helpful for you to know which one of these areas you would like to improve – and reading the chapter of choice in preparation for the lesson will give you tremendous value for your investment. This is not about what you're doing wrong–you're not expected to know this. It's about knowing what's right for you. As a lifetime golfer you will always be working on Contact or Direction, hence, the title of this book... Smash & Carve. Too many players spend time trying to achieve distance. I purposely leave this area alone because if you can achieve skillful contact and direction, distance will naturally develop as a result.

My thoughts for developing this text have been inspired by every lesson, and there have been many over the years. The extensive research I have gathered, combined with constant tinkering in my own game, have contributed greatly to, and inspired the development of Smash & Carve. What I want to address is the incredible similarity of trouble patterns that influence a high majority of golfers. These trouble patterns consist mostly of trying to scoop or pick the ball off the ground, and in trying to create straight shots – Scoop and Straight or Pick and Straight, versus Smash & Carve. These are very different 'styles' of play. Smash & Carve is the ultimate; this style can play anywhere, good lie or bad, wind or no wind. Pick and Straight can play pretty well at times, but struggles with bad lies and trouble shots. Scoop and Straight used by the game's worst players will struggle forever! Smash & Carve is contact and direction. The sole purpose of the swing motion is to develop and perfect, to some degree, these two principle areas in your game. There are two ways to learn and build a golf game; from the swing to the ball, or from the ball to the swing. I want you to build from the ball to the swing to ensure that *function* and *style* are always working together to guarantee steady progress.

lesson 1

Building a Swing

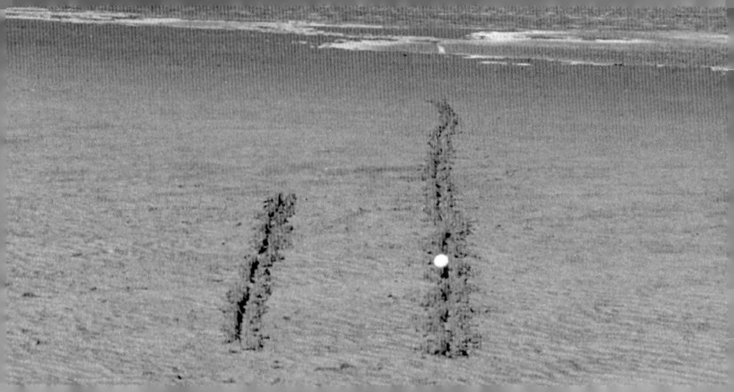

The fundamentals introduced throughout this lesson are the basics. All golfers should be encouraged to learn and develop the basics, regardless of how long it takes for them to feel comfortable. This will ensure a players progress is always moving forward. When a golfer fails to learn the basics completely their progress can become entangled with bad habits that set in, slowing advancement to the next level.

The purpose of this first lesson is to introduce and explore the essential positions and movements in the golf swing. They are: 1. the Grip; 2. the Setup; 3. the Backswing, and; 4. the Unloading sequence. If you consider yourself a player with some experience feel free to skip this lesson and move on to the Smash & Carve lessons 2 and 3. This lesson may be helpful to you later if you need review. If you`re a new golfer with limited experience, it is very important to practice and repeat these basics. Practicing at home (in front of a mirror) with or without a club (similar to shadow boxing) ensures that good habits are being memorized before you begin hitting balls at a driving range.

If a particular position feels awkward or uncomfortable at first, don`t panic, this initial discomfort is quite normal. Constant repetition will ensure these new found habits become natural. The more you can practice the better; be a keener! Eventually these basics will provide you with a dependable foundation to build on in the upcoming lessons.

The Grip

7,8,9 iron or an indoor practice club suggested

The Left Hand

Before you establish your left hand position, the club-face must be square or perpendicular to the intended target line (figure 1).

First: Place your left hand on the club making sure the club face stays in a square position. Extend your left thumb down the grip so it is stretched out (long thumb). Turn your hand slightly to your right so you can see 3 knuckles while looking down (figure 1).

The Right Hand

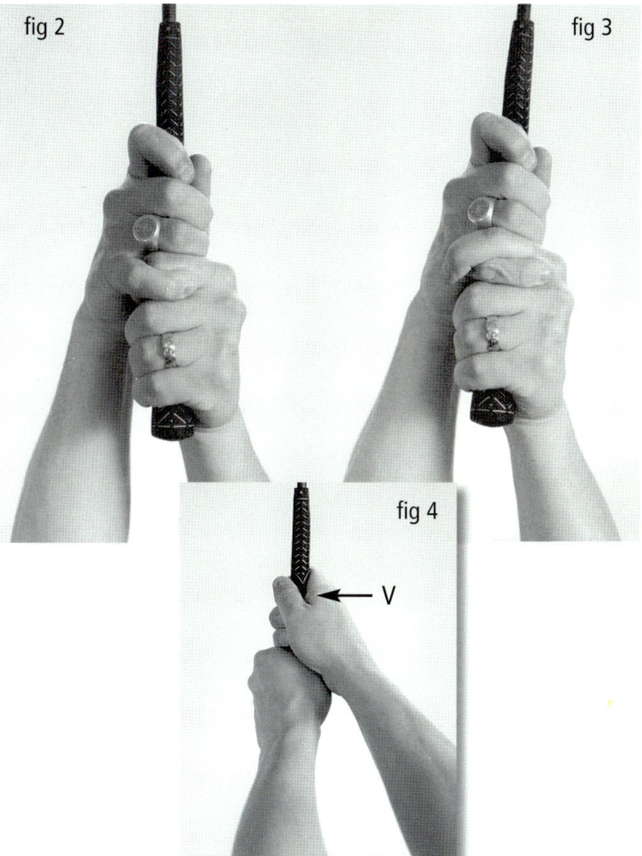

Next: overlap (figure 2) or interlock (figure 3) the right pinky finger with the left forefinger.

Your right hand will complete the grip by closing itself over the thumb on your left hand; the left hand thumb should be completely hidden by the right hand (figure 4). The 'V' of your right hand should point to your chin.

NOTE: The key point when establishing your *right hand* is to hold the club more in the fingers rather than in the palm. This finger hold will allow the completion of the grip to be easily achieved although it may feel awkward for a short time. This initial awkwardness is almost always felt when a golfer insists on remaining strong with their right hand rather than accepting the left hand as dominant. Good golf requires that the left hand be in control, therefore if the right hand initially feels loose and insecure it's a good sign.

The Setup

fig 5

fig 6

The completed set-up from the front angle (figure 5) should consist of:

1. Feet slightly wider than your shoulders.
2. Right foot straight, left foot slightly open (25 degrees approx.).
3. Left arm straight and in line with the club shaft.
4. Right arm bent in toward your stomach.

Ball location will depend on whether you are using an iron club or a wood (figure 6). All iron clubs should be based from 2 inches left of center. All woods should be based off the left heel with a slightly wider stance.

In general longer clubs should be played with a slightly wider stance, and shorter clubs with a slightly narrower stance. Eventually through experience your stance will become more personalized, especially in close to the green. For now, the basics shown above will be sufficient.

fig 7

The completed set-up from the back angle (figure 7) should consist of:

1. Posture
   - -bending from the waist approximately 30 degrees
   - -knees slightly bent, but still tall
   - -butt out, back quite straight
2. Hand position; 6 to 8 inches from your left thigh.

All golf clubs are different lengths so it will be necessary to adjust your distance from the ball. Your posture and hand position (figure 7) should remain constant regardless of how long or short the club is. Simply back up or move closer depending on the chosen club, keeping your hands 6 - 8 inches from the left thigh. Do not stand taller for longer clubs or crouch over for shorter ones. Make your *consistent posture* the strength of your setup.

The Swing Motion

The swing motion consists of: the Backswing, the Downswing, and the Follow-through. Each of these areas need to be treated separately during the developmental stages. As you practice and develop these swing positions you will need to think of your body as two separate sections consisting of INNER PARTS and OUTER PARTS.

fig 8

The INNER PARTS are: the trunk, feet, legs, hips, chest, and head

The OUTER PARTS are (ghosted on the photos above): the shoulders, arms, hands and the golf club)

The backswing sequence will be dominated by the outer parts, mainly the arms.

The downswing sequence will be dominated by the inner parts, mainly the hips.

Centrifugal Force

The foundation of the golf swing is based on centrifugal force. The spinning and uncoiling action from the body will multiply to the arms, then multiply again to the clubhead. For instance, if the hips uncoil at 40mph the arms will travel at 60mph and the clubhead at approximately 80mph. The greater the pulling action from the hips (inner parts) and the transfer of weight, the better. This is true for power *and* control because the arms will have a powerful force (hips) leading them into position.

fig 9

Note: Because centrifugal force is imperative to the swing, I suggest you strengthen your back and stomach. Keep your power center healthy and strong with a stretching program, abdominal exercises (i.e. situps) and back strengthening exercises. Remember, the most important piece of equipment is your body!

The Backswing

The 'loading of the back swing' as it is commonly referred to, is best understood with a heavy emphasis on the word LOADING. When the backswing is done correctly it will load the golfer into a 'spring effect' position. This loaded position is created by a straight left arm (outer parts) that travels much further back than do the hips (inner parts). Loaded means the hips are ready to fire or lead the downswing, that`s why you don`t want your hips to turn very much on the backswing. Indirectly you will be giving your hips a head start by only turning them a fraction of the shoulder turn.

The swing motion begins with a strong set-up position (figure 10) with your left arm dominant and in-line with the club shaft. The initial take-away to the 1/4 position (figure 11) should be dominated with the outer parts, your left arm maintaining dominance (straight). Subtle wrist action to this 1/4 position is two-fold: 1. to fan the clubface open slightly, where the clubface points to the sky (circled in figure11), and; 2. to cock slightly. The inner parts, mainly the hips, remain quite still to this position.

fig 12 fig 13

When moving from the 1/4 position to the 1/2 position (figure 12) the left arm must continue it`s dominance (straight). Your wrists are free to cock more than shown in figure 12 (club shaft vs. left arm is 40° approximate), but I suggest less wrist break rather than more. Your feet should still be flat on the ground, with minimum hip turn (inner parts very quiet).

The completed backswing (figure 13) can stop at approximately the 3/4 position (notice the clubshaft vs. my left arm showing a 90° angle). This is considered to be a complete backswing. Having your left arm travel further past this point will not create extra distance, instead it may decrease your chances for consistency.

The most critical point in the backswing is at the 1/2 position. This is a check point for many advanced players. By setting the club correctly at the 1/2 position, the 3/4 position can then be easily achieved for all body types.

A full backswing (left arm pointing straight up to the sky) is not advisable because of the extra flexibility that is required. Remember, bigger is not necessarily better during the back swing.

The Unloading Sequence

fig 14 fig 15

The unloading sequence consists of the downswing and the follow-through. The change of direction must be dominated with your inner parts. You can spin your hips to the left, or use your right or left leg as a driving force, but whichever you choose, a part of your lower body must initiate the downswing to create the necessary pulling effect that is called centrifugal force. Avoid dominating the unloading process with any of your outer parts for it will only create big problems that lead to even worse habits.

Once the backswing position has been established (figure 14) the unloading sequence can then take place.

The hips (inner parts) are the largest and most powerful part of your body, therefore leading the downswing with the spinning action of your hips will allow your arm swing (outer parts) to drop into a position called the slot (figure 15). The slot is quite close to your right hip and can only be accessed through the correct sequence of movement. On the downswing the inner parts lead and the outer parts follow (refer to pages 18 and 19).

fig 16 fig 17

The follow-through occurs after the ball has been hit, and requires a strong spinning action of the hips combined with the extension of both arms down the target line. Follow through means you swing at the target or down the line. When more power is applied to the shot your arms will travel farther up toward your head.

The only point in the swing where both arms are straight is at the 1/4 follow-through position (figure 16), which is 2 to 3 feet past Impact. The left arm remains straight to this point and the right arm follows suit.

At the 3/4 follow-through position your right arm should remain quite straight (figure 17). Your left arm will begin to fold or bend as the swing nears completion.

Casting

Directly related to the downswing is a common error in movement known as casting. Its cause originates in the first part of the downswing.

Casting means the golfer uncocks the wrists during the downswing (figure 19), thereby failing to control the downswing sequence with their Inner parts. Feeling compelled, the player feverishly tries to hit the ball with the clubhead(Outer Parts). The player casts the clubhead out and away from their body, breaking the correct sequence by not leading the downswing with the lower body spin which, in turn, opens the door to numerous errors. Casting is used when fishing, not golfing, and is an extremely harmful habit that you need to be aware of in the early stages of your development.

At the end of lesson 2 hand action will be covered more extensively. At this point it`s not imperative that you master the correct movement, however you should become familiar with the downswing sequence and the leading action of the lower body spin. Remember that dominating the downswing with the hands and wrists can be disastrous.

fig 18

fig 19

The Power Swing

Your power swing will consist of a 3/4 backswing with a full follow-through. 3/4 to full.

fig 20

fig 21

Greater power is not achieved by increasing your backswing past this 3/4 position (figure 20). Although there are many fine players who do, the fact is bigger is *not* necessarily better! A great example is Tiger Woods; he demonstrates a 3/4 backswing on tour every week. His incredible power does not depend on a full backswing and yet he is arguably the longest hitter in the game.

It is not surprising that a lot of players are almost always concerned with generating more power, but actually golf should be understood as a control game and the premium should be placed on consistency. Everyone has the flexibility to develop a solid 3/4 backswing. Going past this point will not help your consistency or your distance. Balancing the 3/4 follow-through with the 3/4 backswing would be just fine. If you have a lot of acceleration in your unloading process stopping at 3/4 is not advisable. There are many women who can swing over 70 mph and men that can swing over 90 mph, therefore a full follow-through where both arms are bent as the club ends up behind your head (figure 21) is likely to develop. This will depend on how aggressive your nature. Your arms should eventually fold at the follow-through, but not until you are beyond the 3/4 position.

The Game...In Short

In addition to the power swing there are also touch swings that are used to control distance, especially from 100 yards in and around the green. During a round of golf you will encounter different situations that need creativity, especially when distance control is required. You can develop your short game most effectively by learning and practicing 3 touch swings.

There are a wide range of specialty shots in the short game but in this text we will concentrate our efforts on the 1/4 to 1/4, 1/2 to 1/2 and 3/4 to 3/4. Unlike the power swing, the short shot requires the follow-through to mirror the backswing, balancing back to forth. If you take the club back 1/4 way, you follow-through 1/4 way. This is true for the 1/2 and 3/4 swings as well.

The smaller the swing, the shorter distance the ball will travel. As you begin to practice this skill you will also develop a feel that you can rely upon to discern distance. Depending on how the ball is struck a 1/4 swing might produce a 25 yard shot, a 1/2 swing a 50 yard shot and a 3/4 length might hit the ball 75 yards. You will develop feel and consistency through practice and repetition. Eventually, with experience you will be able to control distance through 5 yard increments, 5, 10, 15, 20, etc. Building a repertoire of swing lengths will prepare you for good shot-making at any distance.

quarter to quarter

half to half

three-quarter to three-quarter

Summary

During this lesson we have been developing your basic fundamentals for golf. Do not treat these fundamentals lightly as they will be with you for the rest of your life! I cannot emphasize enough the importance of practicing these basics at home, indoors or outdoors, while watching television, standing in front of a mirror, with or without a club. Go ahead, be a keener, the more the better! You don`t have to be at a driving range to be learning and developing your game.

There are many students that I see in a golf season who do not have the basics established in their muscle memory, therefore improving their game will be a constant struggle because they will always be fighting bad habits. Try to be patient while you learn this multi-faceted game. It requires everyone to learn at a slow and accurate rate so the good habits can develop and become a part of you - to be natural. You can't be in a hurry to learn golf because it takes a lot of time, which is why the best players learned their games while they were young. The main reason kids can improve faster than adults is because they have few responsibilities apart from school and homework. They have all the time to practice and play — what a life! Adults have trouble finding the time between demanding work schedules, spouses and kids. Golf takes patience, practice and time... positive results need to be earned.

Now that you have a good understanding of the basics introduced in this lesson, we will continue to build on these skills in lessons 2 and 3. Lesson 2 (Smash) gives purpose to the swing and explains the technique and importance of contacting the ball properly. Lesson 3 (Carve) explains the shot control focusing on direction. As we move forward, always remember to practice what you've learned in lesson 1 for it is your first step to a successful swing.

Practice...

...Anywhere

...Anytime

lesson 2

CONTACT

My Story of Solid

Definitions

STEP 1 THE CONCEPT

Key Thoughts

STEP 2 FOOTWORK

Don't Keep Your Head Down

STEP 3 ARM EXTENSION

Don't Stay Behind the Ball

STEP 4 THE ARC

Key Thoughts

STEP 5 BALL LOCATION

STEP 6 HAND ACTION

DELAYING VS CASTING

SUMMARY

This lesson will expand on the hitting area, or the Impact zone. The moment of truth – IMPACT! Popular phrases I hear golfers use when describing their well hit shots are, "Did I ever nail that one" or "Was that ever pure!"

Likewise, slang words are often used to describe poorly hit shots, i.e; "oops, chunked that one", and "uh oh, I sculled it". Golfers actually create new words and sayings all the time to describe their performance to themselves and to others. Just recently I heard someone use the word 'squib'. It would benefit you to learn the correct vocabulary now so you can build your ball-striking skills without the confusion of slang terminology.

I will refer to the word SOLID, frequently. It is imperative that you understand this specific word and its meaning as described in this lesson. Solid is the pleasure of the game, the addiction. It is the 'sweet' result of skillful ball striking; the pot at the end of the rainbow. When a golfer can rely on hitting solid shots every time, the game becomes much more enjoyable because consistency has been achieved. Then, distance can be controlled because the ball is being struck consistently, the same way, every time.

IT`S NOT THE DRIVE, IT`S HOW YOU ARRIVE. Many golfers in today`s game are so hung up on hitting the big drive that they disregard the importance of being a solid ball-striker. They think that their driver is the most important club in their bag, when actually the iron clubs are much more significant. That`s why there are more irons than woods in a set of clubs. When a golfer learns how to hit their irons solid, the woods will then be easy to learn. This lesson will concentrate on iron play.

To achieve proficient ball-striking abilities you will have to focus on *impact and the ball to ground relationship*. Learning good ball-striking from the ground up will teach you how your golf swing can produce these solid shots. Without a clear understanding of how the ground relates to impact, even a good swing can produce a picking or scooping action. It is crucial that you build both elements of swing and impact together, thereby achieving SOLID CONTACT.

fig 1 fig 2

These sequence photos show myself using a 7 iron (figures 1 to 4), and I have just hit a solid shot. Notice how the ball and turf are leaving the hitting area. There is certainly a lot of action happening here. Pay particular attention to the angle of the club shaft (figure 2). Notice how it has a backward lean, as my hands are staying out in front of the club-head.

There are many different sayings or phrases that describe this action of Impact you see here. *HIT DOWN AND THROUGH, COMPRESS THE BALL*, or *DE-LOFT THE CLUB.*

All of these phrases effectively describe Impact and the hitting area. They are swing thoughts that have been used by many fine players over the years.

fig 3 fig 4

The action of Impact has varying degrees of aggressiveness and has been described as 'controlled violence'. The size of the divot will depend on certain variables such as the amount of power supplied, the club used, and the condition of the turf. If the shot was only hit 20 yards, the divot will always be quite small. If the club used was a 3 iron from 200 yards, the divot will also be somewhat small. If it was a 9 iron from 140 yards off very wet turf, as is often the case on the west coast, the divot will be huge! Lofted clubs such as 8 iron, 9 iron and wedge tend to take bigger, deeper divots than less lofted clubs. The size of the divot will vary but there will be only one Impact position you are to develop.

The next time you watch a golf tournament on television notice how every player takes divots with their irons. The single most important factor concerning solid is *taking divots*! All good players take them, after they have hit the ball, yet this crucial maneuver goes relatively un-noticed during a player's early years in golf. I want you to learn how the ball gets into the air first, then build the swing fundamentals . In other words, build from the ball to the swing.

my story of solid

I remember vividly the day I discovered how to strike solid shots, the events of which make for an interesting story to share with you. Before continuing, I would like you to keep in mind that I was only 18 years old at the time of this story and, not yet weighed down by the responsibilities of the work world, had a lot of personal time available.

One hot summer afternoon at the old University Golf Course practice fairway, I was practicing alone, wearing out my shag balls with sweaty determination and chasing a dream. I had been playing golf for about 8 years, and a typical summer golf day often lasted from dawn till dusk, hitting as many as a thousand balls. This particular day was, to put it mildly, not going well at all. Disgusted with the way I was striking the ball, my mood turned dark, calling myself every bad name I could think of. Thinking I was useless and pathetic, I lost my temper and started to hit right down on the ball, trying to break my club on it and rip out a huge piece of turf. I would put the ball way back in my stance and smash down on it as hard as possible.

Funny how anger is often a turning point in life, suddenly revealing answers we have struggled for so long to find. Like a silver lining on a very dark cloud, I couldn't believe what started to happen. In absolute awe, I watched shot after shot start with a powerful low trajectory and rise gracefully toward the horizon, reaching its peak before falling to the earth. The whole experience was incredible; I was no longer thinking about swing mechanics, just hitting the ball with a substantial, descending blow. A real smashing action!

All was not yet perfect though. At that time my idol was Jack Nicklaus. I tried to imitate everything he did in his golf game, paying particular attention to the mechanics of the swing. Two very important fundamentals he used, or said he used were: 1. Keep your head still, and 2. Play every shot off your left heel. Up to this time, I used these swing keys religiously, practicing and playing every day. Now, suddenly, I found myself in quite a dilemma. If I played the ball off my left heel and kept my head still as Jack suggested, I could not hit the ball Solid every time but if I played the ball back in my stance and just hit down on the ball I could ~ *What was going on?*

Two years later I found my answer when I was introduced to George Knudson and his theories. In contrast to Jack Nicklaus, George recommended playing the ball in different locations for different irons rather than always off the left heel. He also recommended allowing your head to move during the swing, rather than attempting to keep it still!! This was wonderful news! While I had already figured this out for myself it confirmed that my discovery was right on track. If I had had a clear understanding of Impact from the beginning, I could have saved myself a lot of time, maybe 5 years. *This is exactly what I am trying to do for you—save you time. To help you move forward not backwards.*

There will always be different teaching programs that endorse a variety of concepts. However, one truth will always remain: Good golf absolutely demands SOLID BALL STRIKING. Do you hit solid shots with the swing mechanics you use now?

definitions

Study the definitions below. This is the correct terminology used in describing the contact within the game of golf. Their meanings indicate how (not where) a golfer hits a shot.

SOLID The 'Collins English Language Dictionary' describes something that is solid as having all its individual pieces very close together so there is no space between them.
In golf, the iron club strikes down on the ball, hitting the ball first (solid) then tearing out turf, past the ball, after the ball.

THIN The iron strikes the ball only, without any turf. (An error)

FAT The iron strikes the turf before the ball. (An error)

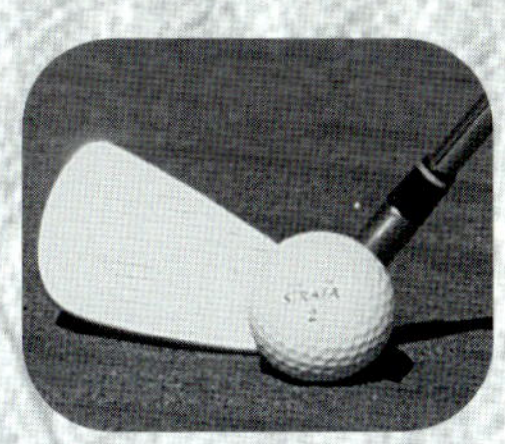

SHANK The iron strikes the ball on the shaft, or the heel area of the club. (An error)

** Toe shots are so rare I have decided not to include them here.*

It is imperative that you memorize and understand these 4 words and their meanings. Without this knowledge your ability to evaluate and communicate your performance is virtually impossible. The following pages are a guide/program toward Solid Ball-striking...these steps deal directly with hitting Solid shots, not with where the ball goes. This we will learn in lesson 3 - direction.

Step 1 ~ The Concept

7,8,9 iron suggested

When learning how to strike a golf ball Solid you must first have the correct impression and vision that deals with the golf club and shaft angle at Impact.

Lets review some important phrases from page 34.

Down and Through - hit the ball on the way down, taking the divot after.

Compress the Ball - getting the clubface to push the ball against the ground

Deloft the Club - hit the ball with your hands ahead of the clubhead.

These three technique phrases describe the same intention — to hit solid shots. They also describe a low trajectory. When trying to achieve solid contact you basically have to like hitting the ball on a lower than normal trajectory (hands ahead of the ball). A good golf swing will tend to *push* the ball out to the target. The loft will then supply the appropriate trajectory. Good ball-strikers get the ball out to the target very fast — they compress the ball against the ground and extend it out to the target all in the same motion.

fig 7

fig 8

Figure 5 shows how the club-head first contacts the golf ball. The initial contact should be (envisioned) in the middle of the ball. Notice how the shaft is leaning to my left, emphasizing delofting with my hands moderately ahead of the ball. Figure 6 shows where the club-head first contacts the ground. Notice how the initial contact is after the ball. The clubhead will then go even further past the ball, tearing out turf as much as 12 to 15 inches past the ball (figure 7). If the hands are not leading the clubhead through the hitting area, taking a divot after the ball is virtually impossible. Let's think for a moment how backspin is created; when the club strikes down on the ball it pinches the ball and compresses it against the ground, the ball then spins out from its compression, riding up the grooves on the clubface producing backspin. The amount of backspin will then depend on 'how much power' and 'what club was used'. There will always be backspin, you don't even have to try for it. A golf shot will never have topspin.

Figure 8 shows how most golfers perceive the hitting area. They try to scoop the ball up. Many believe the higher the shot, the more backspin – this is not the case.

Your first step is to have the correct impression of Impact before proceeding to step #2.

Key Thoughts

Before we look at the golf swing itself and the essentials required to achieve Solid Contact, I would like you to understand that 'taking Divots' with every iron shot you ever hit is imperative! Unfortunately, most golf facilities in areas where the game is seasonal only allow golfers to hit practice balls from mats – talk about different! You play the game off grass yet you have to practice off mats! If the thought of hitting the ground is not at the top of your list, it will always be difficult to hit the ball solid and experience the pleasure of it. As your ball striking improves you will learn to appreciate and eventually enjoy striking the ground and taking divots. Reinforce this point weekly by watching golf on television. If the best players take divots, why shouldn't you?

It`s important to note that power is not required at this point in time. The easiest way to build proper contact and become a better player is by practicing smaller shots that are inside 100 yards – pitching and chipping. This will allow your body to absorb the impact of a golf shot without risking injury to yourself. Do not disregard the importance of practicing the short game more than your power game; don't forget that the point of the game is to get the ball in the hole!

1/4 to 1/4 and 1/2 to 1/2 These swings are as big as you will need to start developing proper contact. The larger your swing gets, the more difficult hitting solid shots will become. Power has its place in the game, but remember that consistency is the key to improving. Learning the game from your short shots is a win-win situation; you will develop your short game and become a solid ball-striker. The full-swing is a mere extension of the 1/2 swing, the ball-striking basics are the same. There is only one description of proper contact, whether it be a 10 yard shot with a pitching wedge or a 180 yard shot with a 5 iron, the shots get hit the exact same way – SOLID!

The image below shows a divot pattern after 100 balls have been hit with a 7-iron. The grid illustration shows the order with which the pattern is created. Taking pride in your divot pattern will promote consistency in your ball-striking and is easily repaired.

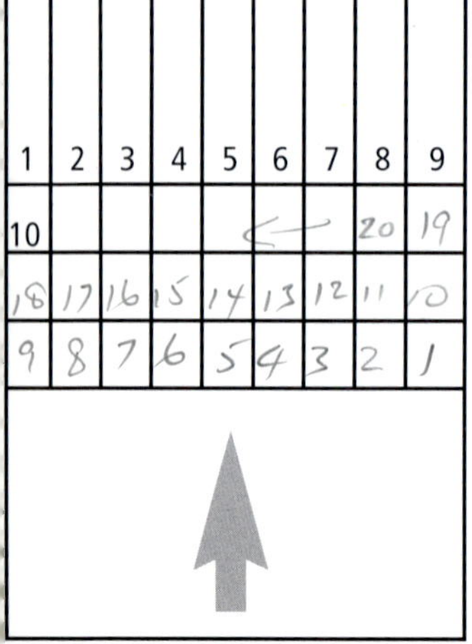

Step 2 ~ Footwork *the weight shift*

When hitting Solid golf shots a player must dominate the swing motion with the Inner Parts. The weight-shift (inner parts) is the foundation of any good golf swing and must be the dominant force before attention can be focused on the arms and hands. Many struggling golfers dominate the golf swing with their arms and don`t use nearly enough hips and legs during the unloading process.

When loading the backswing (figure 9) your feet should stay flat on the ground (don`t lift your left heel). Your hip turn should be minimal, with only a slight weight-shift to the right. By keeping your feet flat on the ground, your body will be 'coiling' or loading. You might feel a little stiffness in your lower back caused by your feet staying flat on the ground. This stiffness is necessary, that`s what is meant by 'loading'; you load up your right side, readying it to spring forward.

When unloading the downswing and follow-through, your hips and your legs must go first. The center, which is dominated by the weight-shift and spinning action of your body (figure 10) will pull your arms through the hitting area and into the follow-through (figure 11). Notice the complete turn of the hips to face the target.

In my opinion, if there was a most important move in the golf swing it would have to be the weight-shift. There has to be a dominant force in the swing motion, and that dominant force is controlled by the weight-shift.

fig 9

fig 10

fig 11

Don't keep your head down

fig 12

As your body weight shifts naturally and aggressively to your left foot do not keep your head down; in fact, this swing thought should be banished from the game. It will only hinder progress, not help it! Annika Sorenstam of the LPGA Tour and David Duval of the PGA Tour have been helpful examples of just how early a player can lift their head once they have hit the ball. They keep their heads quite still on the backswing, but on the downswing and follow-through they appear to be leading with their face and lifting their head almost before contact. This type of swing action is just wonderful because it dismisses that age old rule that 'you have to keep your head down'. Not only will this tip limit your progress and make you feel and look completely un-natural, it is very damaging to your back and neck muscles (figure 13).

Practice becoming more of a ***tall player***. The strength and grace of a good swing comes from being tall. Lift your head right after you hit it, and stand very tall at the follow-through. It is still very possible to take divots and be tall, it just requires practice.

This 'old school' cliché is also not in agreement with modern kinesthetic knowledge; it won't help your swing and you could injure yourself – don`t be influenced by it.

fig 13

Step 3 ~ Arm Extension

The downswing to slightly post-impact is considered the 'moment of truth'. Our efforts will concentrate on this 'attack of the ball'.

At Impact 90% of your body weight must be on your left foot showing the domination from the weight-shift (figure 14). Your left arm should still be quite straight, your right arm slightly bent, BUT DRIVING THE CLUB FORWARD AS IT STRAIGHTENS

Your left arm should continue to drive through the hitting area, staying ahead of your right arm. This left arm extension will provide the 'divot action' after Impact (figure 15).

Approximately 2 feet past impact your right arm should finally straighten (figure 16). This is the only point in the swing that both arms are fully extended.

The left arm is in control of the post-impact extension of both arms. If the left arm is extending down the line, the right can't help but extend also. The left arm must always dominate the right, which might be the reason why the glove is worn on the left hand.

Down and Through describes a technique that should be practiced religiously. This swing thought can single-handedly promote ball striking excellence and make the *solid* shot a consistent part of your game.

fig 14

fig 15

fig 16

Note: the slight backward bend of the left wrist in figure 16 is a result of the action called Supination. When combined with the left arm extension, it will lengthen the hitting area tremendously. Supination is discussed at length in lesson 4.

Don't stay behind the ball

fig 17

When extending your left arm out toward the target, thus taking your divots after the ball, you may lose your balance toward the target from time to time (figure 17). If this happens don`t panic, it`s not as bad as you might think. In losing your balance toward the target you are reinforcing the thought of taking the divot after the ball.

Gary Player has been an excellent example over the last 4 decades of a great player that doesn`t stay behind the ball, in fact he actually takes a couple of steps toward the target after hitting the ball. If anything, he falls forward, getting his entire body weight into the shot. It`s a wonderful swing move to imitate.

fig 18

Ideally, at the completion of the swing (figure 18) you would like to be standing straight up, over your left foot, facing the target with perfect balance.

Avoid the loathsome 'C-Back' (figure 19). This position is commonly achieved by players that believe in either keeping their head still throughout the swing, or staying behind the ball. You can probably imagine from the photo that this is not a very comfortable position. Please protect your back and neck area – swing healthy!

fig 19

Step 4 ~ The Arc

The back and forward arc of the swing motion will be different on either side of the ball.

On the backswing (figure 20, solid line) the left arm arc should be quite wide. Your left arm extension should be full, away from your body, keeping the inner parts quite still.

On the downswing (figure 21, dotted line) the arc should shrink somewhat. Your arms should be pulled into your body slightly, as your weight-shift begins to pull your arms down. On the downswing, your arms should get considerably closer to your body, creating a steeper descending angle than that of the back-swing.

On the follow-through (figure 22) the arc will extend out again, just like the backswing. This arc change only re-affirms the swing key of 'down and through'.

In short, the swing arc should be: Wide, then shallow, then wide.

When practicing the swing arc and the previous steps, remember the eventual goal of hitting 'Solid shots' and taking divots after the ball.

fig 20

fig 21

fig 22

Key Thoughts

Before continuing, I would like to share some interesting perceptions of contact that many golfers have. One of my main goals of this text is to put forth a clear understanding of Impact and how the ball gets into the air. A clear majority of all golfers I teach in a season have very similar perceptions of Impact and most of the time these perceptions are damaging. Here are a few examples:

·I`M AIMING TO HIT THE GROUND *JUST BEFORE* THE BALL

·THE CLUB *SCOOPS AND LIFTS* THE BALL INTO THE AIR

·I MUST *GET UNDER* IT

These thoughts are very damaging; they have nothing to do with hitting solid shots. They are opposites of the 'down and through' action you are learning. If you relate to statements such as these, I firmly believe it will be impossible to develop solid contact because misdirected statements such as these will stop your learning curve from moving forward.

These types of evaluation statements are so popular with the average golfing population it`s no wonder over 80% of all golfers shoot over 100! If you are a fairly new golfer you don`t have to feel bad, these damaging statements are made even by decent players with over 10 years of experience.

Make sure that statements you make are accurate in explaining your shots and your game. If I heard a student of mine say, "I`m just not getting under it," it would always be a struggle for that student to improve. Almost every student I teach is simply amazed when I hit an iron shot and show them the divot after the ball, they can`t believe it. It seems to be information that isn`t being talked about nearly enough. So remember, hit down on the ball with a descending blow and take the divot after the ball – DOWN AND THROUGH!

Step 5 ~ Ball Location

As you gain more experience with golf you will find that 'where' you place the ball in relation to your stance is an on-going process, there are no absolutes; there are only recommendations. The more advanced your game, the more variations in ball location. I will give you a base to work from, but also encourage you to experiment.

fig 23

The main difference in a set of golf clubs is between woods and irons. The woods are designed to sweep the ball into the air, where the irons are designed to take divots. It is because of this design difference, that your ball location should change. A standard ball location for hitting woods is off your left heel (figure 23) or forward in your stance. A standard ball location for hitting irons is; in the center of your stance (figure 24) or slightly left of center (no more than 2 inches).

Because in this lesson we are not dealing with hitting woods, I will encourage you to experiment with putting the ball back in your stance with your irons. Try placing the ball 2 inches right of center, then 4 inches right of center, then 6 inches right of center, etc. Notice how different ball locations create different trajectories – have fun while you experiment.

fig 24

Step 6 ~ Wrist Action

Before we get into step 6, I would like you to understand that the correct Hand Action (wrist action) is developing in your swing motion as a result of studying and practising the previous 5 steps. If you feel that your contact is improving, then you need not practice this step *at this time*.

fig 25

fig 26

The essential elements for correct hand action during the swing motion

1. *Understanding the word Solid and how the club-head must deloft at Impact.*
2. *The weight-shift moving forward to your left foot must be strong enough to assist the delofting process.*
3. *The left arm extension must drive down and through, down the line, not up at the sky.*
4. *The arc must shrink as the downswing begins, the left arm extension should be quite wide going back, then on the down swing the arc will get considerably closer to the body, before extending away from the body again after Impact.*
5. *Ball location will effect the delofting process.*

Our final step is to train the wrists to *lag the clubhead* during the downswing. This final step deals with 'backward momentum'. The clubhead must stay behind the hands at Impact in order to maximize the velocity of speed through the hitting zone. If the clubhead catches up to the hands at any point in the downswing the 'stored up power' will be lost and a nasty scooping action will develop.

While you are developing *flowing* hand action it is very important to be aware of when and where the wrist break is needed. On the back swing very little wrist-break is needed; wrist action is needed in the downswing just before impact. Basically, more delay means more power.

Notice in figures 25 and 26 how the wrist-break in my backswing is minimal (70 degrees approximate). On the downswing the wrists should break backwards, delaying the clubhead (figures 27 and 28). A similar movement takes place when 'raking the grass', it`s a pulling action. This pulling action is also known as the 'lagging action'.

fig 27

fig 28

Figure 28 demonstrates how the wrists remain delayed until they reach the golf ball. This 'late release' must be trusted in the early going as shots flying high to the right should be expected.The correct lagging action from the wrist combined with a strong weight shift to your left foot creates the stored up power that propels the ball. This delay action when combined with the backward bend from the clubshaft (backward momentum) will deliver maximum clubhead speed.

DELAY THE HIT, WAIT FOR IT – these swing keys explain the lagging action. When the weight-shift is strong to the left foot and the wrists are delaying on the downswing you will be amazed at how far you are able to hit a ball.

This particular swing move is considered by many to be very frustrating. Because the clubhead gets sort of 'left behind' many will panic; they feel a sense of 'not knowing where the clubhead is'. Actually, the clubhead will be where it should be – following your body.

The lagging action is not only necessary for power and control reasons, it will also apply to your short shots in close to the green. Also known as *soft hands,* the lagging action is needed for touch as well.

Delaying vs Casting

Errors have a way of creating a dominos effect in the golf swing, and Casting is no exception. Often originating with an incorrect perception of impact, *casting relates to getting under the ball and scooping* (figure 32). Notions of having to retrace the swing arc, back and down, and not getting off the right side through impact, can both be isolated causes of casting. Casting often develops out of a combination of bad habits. It completely opposes the 'lagging action' that is necessary to create the proper flow and delay from the wrists during the downswing (figures 29 & 30).

On the previous page notice the near 70° wrist break in figure 26 (top of backswing). If the wrists uncock on the downswing (figure 31) there wouldn't have been much point in cocking them to begin with. This would mean the wrists cocked and uncocked before the ball was hit, resulting in two unnecessary moves.

Casting is defeating the purpose of using equipment that will flex. By attempting to hit *down and through* on all iron shots you will remove most of the tendencies to cast. Stay clear of this frequent error common among pickers and scoopers.

Summary

Contact is such a necessary element in the game of golf, first because it gets the ball air-born and second because it allows the player to control the distance. Controlling the distance is the essence of the game. The result of good contact is 'solid' and this should apply to all the irons, short game included. Solid is set out for you to learn and earn by focusing on this lesson, but while practicing you may find yourself falling prey to a vicious circle that involves hitting fat and thin shots alternately. If you happen to hit a few fat shots while practicing *don't assume that you've hit too much ground* – you've actually hit too far behind the ball. Because you fear gouging too much earth again you are apt to hit the next shot thin, intentionally avoiding the ground. This is the vicious circle: fat, thin, fat, thin etc. They are opposites of each other.

By providing you with a clear understanding of the importance of 'impact', and giving you the goal of 'solid', you should now be able to apply these steps to a practice program and ready yourself for mastering this lesson; it shows you how to achieve the true objective... to SMASH! Now, on to.....CARVE!

lesson 3

DIRECTION

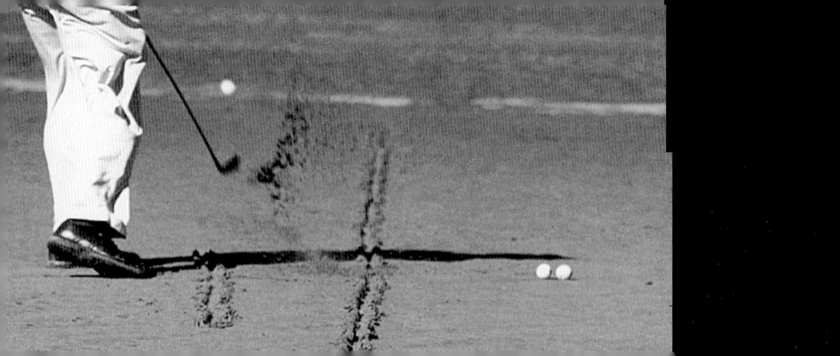

In this lesson we will explore the *DIRECTION* and *FLIGHT* of the golf ball. Similar to lesson 2, I suggest you memorize the terminology and shot patterns that deal with direction. It is important that these descriptions be second nature in your mind in order to avoid getting easily confused.

This lesson is not more significant than lesson 2-Contact – it is secondary because you must be able to contact the ball Solid consistently before you can practice your direction effectively. Every golfer will work on direction for the rest of their lives! Therefore, you must take care of the contact first.

The direction in which a golf ball flies is influenced by *spin*. The ball is always spinning. Every golf shot you will ever hit will have back-spin and side-spin, unless there is no power. The back-spin will not be our concern because when the ball is hit solid, the grooves, which are cut into all irons, produce the back spin. Our concern will be the 2 side-spins. The side spin action is made up of two directions; *CLOCK WISE* and *COUNTER CLOCK WISE*. Clock wise produces a slice spin and counter clock wise produces a hook spin; *STRAIGHT* spin can happen purely by chance or through the intentions of an advanced ball striker. At this point, you should work to eliminate the thought of straight, it will only impede your progress.

Golf is similar to various other sports and activities involving an object, where the technique that is used determines how the object flies. In baseball, a pitcher uses a variety of spins to produce curveballs, sinkers, and sliders. In tennis a player applies top, bottom, and side spins. In billiards players use a variety of side-spins and top and bottom spins as well. Try throwing a frisbee sometime, it slices and hooks just like a golf ball. In golf you only have to worry about clock-wise and counter-clock-wise spin, the back-spin takes care of itself.

Golf's 2 Sidespins

USABLE CLOCKWISE SPIN: produces pull-fade & pull-slice.
Also known as left to right.

USABLE COUNTER CLOCKWISE SPIN: produces push-draw & push-hook.
Also known as right to left.

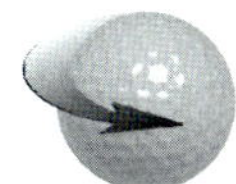

The remainder of lesson 3 will focus on the swing mechanics which relate to the 4 positive shot patterns

The 4 Negative Shot Patterns

These four shot patterns are unusable.
Be aware of them for evaluation purposes only.

The pages ahead will guide you toward developing these four shots patterns.

For the remainder of this lesson, clockwise & counter clockwise spins will refer only to the usable

clockwise spin

fig 1

Notice in the 'action photo' (figure 1) how my ball is taking off to the left of the target line. This initial take-off is called a *PULL*. The bending arrow is showing the ball flight through the air, that being a *FADE*. If the ball flight shows a small curve, it is referred to as a fade. If the ball flight shows a big curve it is referred to as a slice (pull-fade or pull-slice). This particular ball flight is also referred to as *LEFT to RIGHT*. My ball has started left of the target, then is fading to the right.

counter clockwise spin

fig 2

Notice in the 'action photo' (figure 2) how my ball is taking off to the right of the target line. This initial take-off is called a *PUSH*. The bending arrow is showing the ball flight through the air, that being a *DRAW*. If the ball flight shows a small curve, it is referred to as a draw. If the ball flight shows a big curve it is referred to as a hook (push-draw or push-hook). This particular ball flight is also referred to as *RIGHT to LEFT*. My ball has started right of the target, then is drawing to the left.

You will be developing this ball flight initially because over 90% of all golfers are slicers. The right to left shot follows this page.

Right to Left

The counter clockwise spinning action in a right to left shot produces a push-draw or a push-hook. Before you learn the 'release' you must first be able to visualize the required spin that is needed. Through this next process you will learn how to put a *COUNTER CLOCK-WISE* spin on the ball. This process is broken down into *4 steps*. The *'release'* will teach you to hit the ball to the left; the *grip* will teach you to hit the ball more to the left. The *swing-path* will teach you how to hit the ball to the right, and the *alignment* will teach you how to hit the ball further to the right. Together these steps will deliver right to left direction with big shape or small shape resulting in a push-hook or a push-draw.

Step 1 ~ The Release

As you are moving the club-head through the hitting area there is a movement called the release. The release can also be called 'the roll-over' or 'toe up to toe up'. The release happens at the bottom of the swing, approximately 2 feet before the ball to 2 feet after the ball; this is called the *hitting area*. When entering the hitting area your club-face should be in a slightly *open* position (figure 3). When moving through this area your club-face should gradually *close* (figure 4). This *open to closed* movement is called the *release*. The release is a very natural and powerful movement to eventually be controlled by the left hand, left wrist, and left forearm (discussed further in lesson 4).

fig 3

fig 4

As you are practicing the release by rolling your wrists over, visualize the golf ball spinning when you hit it — keep visualizing the counter clockwise spin.

When hitting full shots, the release will happen so fast it will be a blur. Since many male players can swing the club over 90 miles per hour, it's easy to see why it is a split second event.

Step 2 ~ The Strong Grip

Once you have established the release, the grip becomes a very important fundamental. The strength of your left hand grip controls the release. The strength of your grip is determined by your *LEFT HAND KNUCKLES* (not by how tight you hold the club). How many knuckles can you see on your left hand while standing at attention, looking down? If you can see 3 or 4 knuckles this is quite a strong grip (figure 5).

The number of knuckles you show on your left hand will control the release that happens through the hitting area. For example: if you wanted to hook the ball an extreme amount you would strengthen your grip to 4 knuckles. If you wanted to draw the ball slightly, you might only show 2 knuckles. I strongly encourage you to experiment with different strengths. Show 4 knuckles, 3½, 3 knuckles, 2½ and so on. By experimenting you are developing an arsenal of weapons to help you overcome the obstacles that are a part of the game – this is shot-making!

By using a strong grip as recommended you should be able to see your ball *HOOK*. Now it will probably be a pull-hook (refer to page 56), but at this time any hook is a good hook.

Please understand that we are building the right to left shot. Direction to the left is controlled by the combination of *a strong grip and the release*. Now we will develop inside-out, which delivers direction to the right.

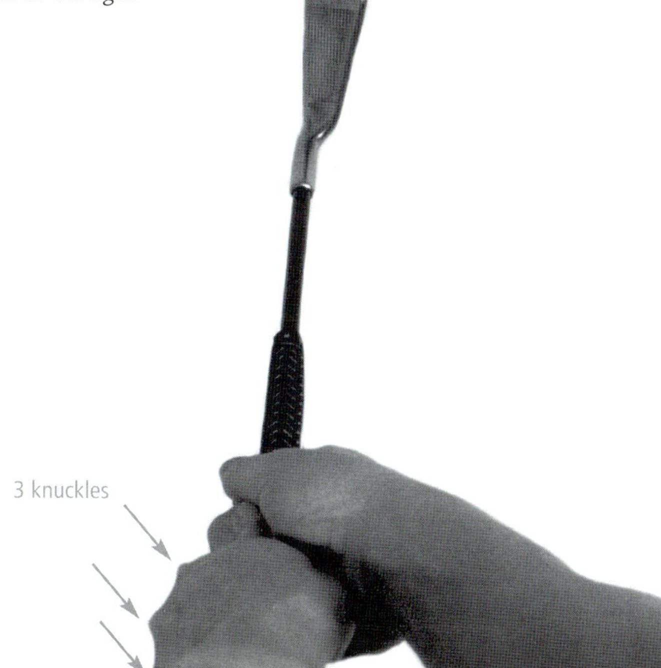

fig 5

Step 3 ~ Inside Out

fig 6

fig 8

fig 9

Developing an 'inside-out swing path' will complete the fundamental movements required in delivering a right to left golf shot – it is essential that the shot starts to the right of the target then works left with spin (thus right to left).

On the backswing (figure 8) a straight take-away is always preferable. The back-swing should travel more toward the sky (upright), rather than around your body (flat).

On the downswing the hips must always initiate; they will always lead and pull your arms downward. Learn how to loop the club behind you at the start of the downswing, training the arms and hands to be pulled down by the right hip. Your hands might even brush against the right hip pocket (figure 9). Eventually a strong weight shift and hip turn to the left will automatically drop the arms into this position – also known as the slot.

Step 3 ~ Inside Out

fig 7

fig 10

fig 11

Inside-out is easy to understand when relating the downswing to a clock. The *backswing* will draw back at 6 o'clock or straight back (figure 8). The *downswing* must loop the club to the inside as to be attacking the ball from 7 o'clock (figure 6 & 10). The *follow-through* must continue on this established angle traveling out to 1 o'clock (figure 7 & 11).

This is the inside-out action; a straight take-away, loop the club to the inside on the way down, swing your arms out and away from you on an angle described by 7 o'clock to 1 o'clock (downswing & follow-through only).

This inside-out swing path must then coordinate with the release of the wrists to produce the required counter clockwise spin on the ball, thus delivering a right to left shot. Many people experience difficulty incorporating this move into their swing; give it a chance and you will be amazed at what it will accomplish!

Key Thoughts

The release, the strong grip and the inside-out swing path must work together to achieve a right to left golf shot. Acting alone, any one of these principles will not deliver the desired shot pattern. However, practicing them separately until you can manage them together will produce quicker results. It is necessary to master these fundamentals if you want to produce greater distance in your game – it is the right to left shot that generates extra power.

Long hitters especially adhere to these fundamentals. Tiger Woods, John Daly and Laura Davies are among the longest hitters in the game today and all three have very similar right to left fundamentals as discussed in this lesson.

The right to left shot can be the most difficult curvature to learn amongst average golfers and although it may not be easy to swing from the inside-out and release the wrists, it is the healthiest natural swing for the body. If you can hit a large right to left shot, your swing must be pretty good! Remember that golf is a shot-makers game and without this vital directional approach to your practice you may very well end up in the 90% of golfers who remain slicers!!

Step 4 ~ Alignment

As you are practicing your right to left shots using a full release, combined with a strong grip as well as an inside-out swing path, you don`t have to aim at anything in particular. I would like you to use the entire right side of the driving range. Your alignment will depend on how excessive you want your hook or draw to be.

Short irons are good clubs for practicing hook shape; long irons and woods are difficult to hook. Practice a variety of curves such as; your biggest hook, your smallest hook, and a somewhere in between hook. Aim 20 yards right, 30 yards right, 50, 60 and so on. Also strengthen your grip accordingly; 2 knuckles, 2½, 3, 3½, 4. Have some fun experimenting! See if you can just miss the right fence line at your range, then bend the ball with a really large curve back to the left. Practice shaping your ball right to left with a variety of curves. Doing this will add fun to an otherwise tedious practice routine, and will help you to familiarize yourself with your ability to *carve* the ball. Always remember the two basic shots are draw and hook. The better players in this game can control their shape in 5 yard increments. For example: 5 yard draw, 10, 15, 20 etc. Your shotmaking skills will always be tested during a round of golf; the more control you have over shape the more you will be able to fit a shot to a situation.

Practicing a variety of curves is not only positive for your game but is also a lot of fun. You're allowed to have fun while learning this game of a lifetime. The fun is in the shot-making!

Left to Right

Before I introduce step 1, try to visualize the spin that is needed to produce a left to right shot. These next 4 steps will promote the *left to right* shot and the fundamentals that are required to produce *CLOCKWISE SPIN*. These steps are *opposites* from the 4 steps that control counter clockwise spin.

Before proceeding, it is important to understand that slicing a golf ball becomes more pronounced as loft diminishes. For example: a driver will tend to slice more than a 5-wood; a 5-iron will tend to slice more than a 9-iron. In general, the longer the club, the bigger the slice.

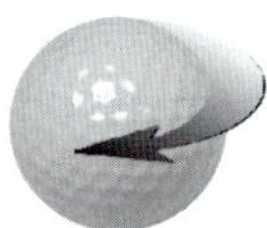

Step 1 ~ No Release

When understanding the proper release that is required to hit a slice (fade) or a left to right shot, the first thing to realize is that *there is no release*. It is because of a lack of release that so many players slice the ball – if there is no wrist roll through the hitting area the shot is called 'a block'. The big difference between a hook and a slice is that you roll your wrists to hook (closing the clubface), you don`t roll your wrists to slice (clubface stays open, figure 14). As you are practicing this blocking action by not rolling your hands through the hitting area, notice the ball spinning clockwise. The ball will probably go directly to the right because the clubface is still open. When hitting *slices* the clubface must stay open. When hitting *hooks* the clubface must close. You either block or release with your hands through the hitting area.

fig 13

fig 14

Step 2 ~ The Weak Grip

The weakening of your left hand grip will control the blocking action at impact. Blocking at impact will leave the clubface open, thereby making the golf ball spin clockwise because your wrists won`t be able to roll over from this weak grip position. A weak grip will have you standing at attention, looking down, being able to see 1 or 2 knuckles on your left hand (figure 15).

I strongly suggest you experiment with the weakness of your left hand grip; you should be able to show a 1 knuckle grip and a 2 knuckle grip. These two grips relate to the 2 basic shots you are trying to learn how to hit; the fade and the slice, or left to right.

The weak grip may not be as important as the strong grip because so many golfers already have trouble with slicing. Practicing the slice, or the fade, is still healthy practice and will not pose a problem as long as you understand the fundamentals that control the shot.

Please understand that we are building the left to right shot. Direction to the right is controlled by the combination of *a weak grip and no release*. Now we will develop *outside-in*, which delivers direction to the left.

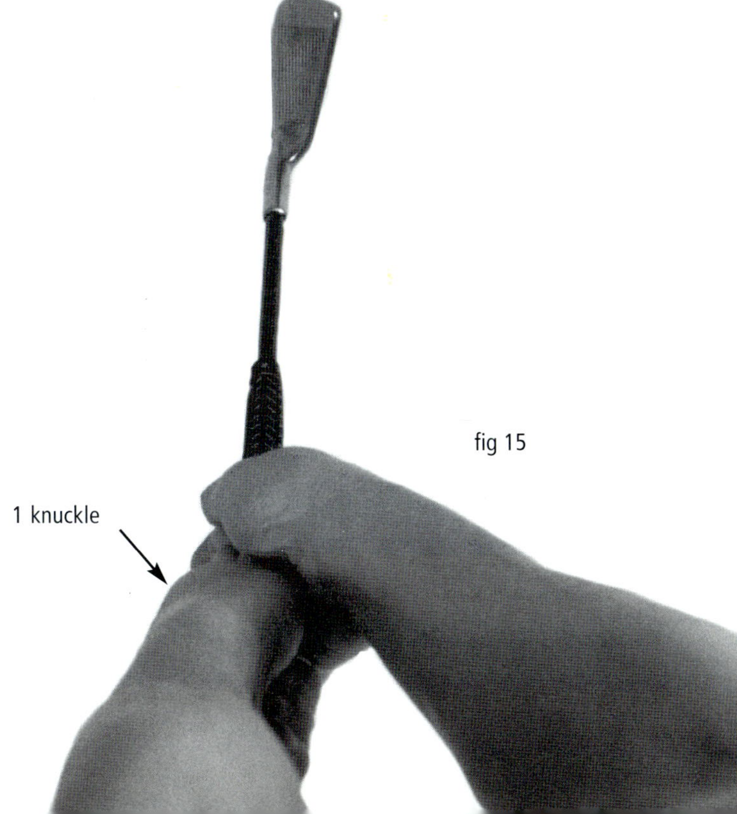

fig 15

Step 3 ~ Outside In

fig 16

fig 18

fig 19

An outside-in swing path is a very common swing move shared by many struggling golfers. Considering that most golfers slice, it is a foregone conclusion that most golfers swing from the outside-in. This swing move is considered a flaw for a golfer that can`t hit from the inside-out. Ideally, the complete player could perform both swing paths on command; they would be able to swing from the outside-in and from the inside-out.

Again the straight take-away (figure 18) will always be preferable. On the *downswing*, a transition loop opposite of 'inside-out' is made (figure 19).

Step 3 ~ Outside In

fig 17

fig 20

fig 21

Outside-in is easy to understand when relating the downswing to a clock. Your *backswing* will get drawn back at 6 o'clock or straight back (figure 18). Your *downswing* will loop the club, to the outside, thereby attacking the ball from 5 o'clock (figure 16 & 20). Your *follow-through* will continue on this established angle traveling past the ball to 11 o'clock (figure 17 & 21).

Outside-in is also referred to as 'over the top' and considered by many to be an error. However if this swing move is used intentionally it can add a new dimension to your shotmaking. Having the ability to carve the ball using *both swing paths* will provide you with an almost limitless repertoire of shots using the full range of the swing plane.

Step 4 ~ Alignment

As you are practicing these left to right shots using the weaker left hand grip, combined with an outside-in swing path, you don`t have to aim at anything in particular. I would like you to use the entire left side of the driving range, as opposed to the right side we were using to practice the right to left shot. Your alignment will depend on the club you choose and how excessive you want the slice or fade to be. A good club selection for practicing your slice shape would be a 5-iron. When practicing your left to right shape it is okay to go down in club selection because the shot will tend to go much higher than right to left. Hooks will generally fly quite low and slices tend to fly much higher (do you understand why?). Practice a variety of curves, starting with the biggest slice you have. See if you can just miss the left fence line at your range, then bending the ball back to the right. Practice big and small left to right shape using the fundamentals of the weak grip/outside-in swing path and aiming varying degrees to the left. However, be careful with this shot as you could just aim left and by using your normal swing, have the ball slice all by itself. In general, most golfers should almost exclusively practice the right to left shot.

fig 22

Summary

In conclusion to this lesson on direction and the swing fundamentals that control the flight of the ball, remember that golf is a shotmaker's game and your ability to control the direction will add considerably to your confidence. Considering that the straight shot is an advanced one, it is imperative that you concentrate your efforts on improving your weaknesses first. The four basic shots are: draw, hook, fade and slice. Practicing big and small, left to right and right to left shape using a variety of curvatures will help you to understand how clockwise and counter clockwise spin effects the ball flight. Until you have developed a good understanding and basic ability to execute these shots on command it is best to leave the straight shot to the pros.

You may need to change your expectations and thoughts dealing with direction. Often I hear a new student say, "I just want to hit it straight". Actually, this is a very advanced skill, and it is the opposite that is easier and more productive for your overall game – learn to be a good shotmaker. While you are still learning, if you have trouble hitting a shot right to left, then play left to right when it really matters. Work on the weak parts of your game until they are strong enough to play on the course.

lesson 4

Supination

In lessons two and three, Smash and Carve were studied separately, explaining their intent and purpose to contact and direct the ball. You might expect then that the next lesson would be on distance.

"How can I hit the ball farther? Power is everything; without it I can't improve." While these thoughts may have some truth to them, it is how that power is achieved that will ultimately affect your game. Separately, Smash and Carve relate to contact and direction, but they are linked together by one word – *Supination.**

Supination is rarely taught or talked about and this may be why I hear golfers say, "those teachers don`t really tell you everything." It might be golf's greatest secret because nobody seems to know what it means or how it relates to golf shot performance. Therefore, the purpose of lesson 4 will be to give a clear explanation of this very powerful word and dispel the mystery that separates the extraordinary player from a student that feels excluded from the 'secrets'.

In this lesson I will also explain the differences between Supination and Pronation, and their roles in the swing motion. On more than one occasion I have heard students say, "this is what the pros know, huh?" In addition, I will discuss one of the most common hurdles for the learning golfer to overcome – the dreaded 'shanks'. If Supination has been a secret and Shanking has been hidden in the closet, this lesson will shed some much needed light in both directions.

*Hogan, Ben. Five lessons. The Modern Fundamentals of Golf

Supination happens at impact and beyond (figures 2,3 and 4), and refers to the function of the left hand, left wrist, and left forearm only. In order to practice this significant action effectively, a dominant weight shift to the left foot is mandatory.

fig 1

fig 2

fig 3 fig 4

The function of the right hand and right arm *will not be discussed at all* during this lesson, the reason being that the right hand and arm must always follow the leading left. Even though my right hand appears to overtake my left in figure 4, I am actually focused *only on keeping my left hand and arm leading.* The right (bottom hand) is so powerful it never needs to be exercised or stressed. If and when the right is dominating, poor results are sure to follow.

Pronation vs. Supination

Definitions from Webster`s Illustrated Dictionary:

Pronation · To turn the palm of the hand (or inner surface of a forelimb) downward or backward.

In golf this movement is needed during the backswing and downswing. Essentially, pre-impact involves left hand pronation.

Supination · To turn the palm and forearm upward.

In golf this movement is needed at impact and beyond. Essentially, post-impact involves left hand supination

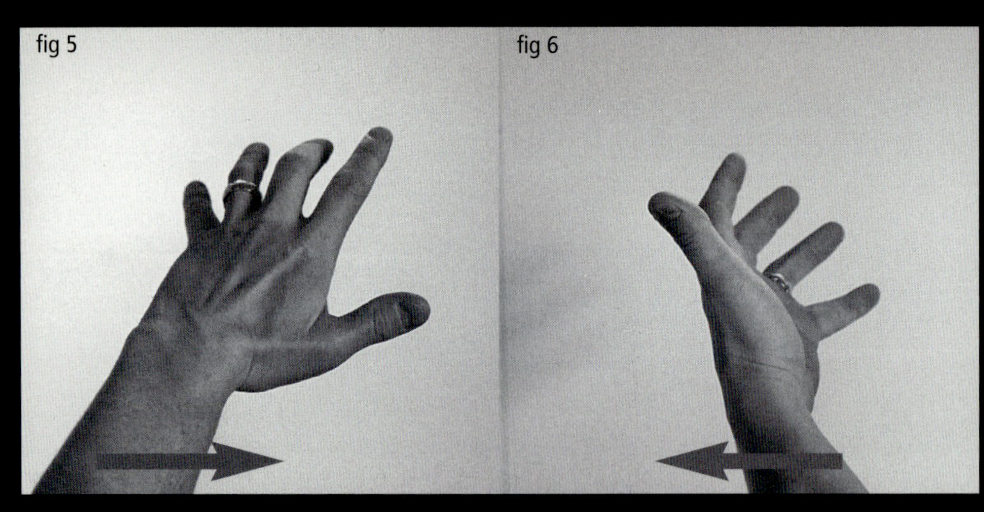
fig 5
fig 6

I strongly encourage you to practice this left handed movement without a club as much as possible. Air Swings can be practiced anytime and will build coordination, memory and strength into the preferable dominant side.

Practicing with your right hand and right arm is *not necessary because the left must always control the right*. Start strengthening your left side as soon as possible.

fig 7

When swinging a golf club, the transition from Pronation to Supination can happen quickly or slowly depending on how much power is applied. This action happens just-before-impact-till-just-after-impact. The tighter this movement surrounds the ball the better.

Supination is two-fold. To understand it fully we have to break it down into two separate areas; Directional Supination and Contact Supination.

Directional Supination

Please refer to figure 7 and notice how the left hand rolls-the-club-face-over through the hitting area, showing the palm of the left hand to the player. This is Directional Supination. Initially this movement was discussed in lesson 3 (right to left golf shots). The 'left hand Release' is also known as Directional Supination and when combined with the strength of the left hand knuckles, the more the club-face will close during the hitting area. If the left hand Supination through impact is too great, creating too much hook, then weakening the left hand knuckles is required. Chances are this will not be the case if you take into consideration that so many golfers slice the ball. Supination is a standard, you must work with it, not against it, on all shots. Slicers try to keep the club-face straight or square, steering through impact rather than developing and trusting the 'roll-over action'. These are two very different schools of thought. In order to experience the natural power of release you must let go of the notion that the club-face stays straight through impact. The only sure way to effectively control the club-face is through left hand Supination.

Contact Supination

During the roll-over action as shown in figure 7 (previous page) the left wrist must also 'bow' or lean forward through impact. This bending of the left wrist toward the target will deloft the clubface and allow the palm of the left hand to be seen by the player (fig 8). This is Contact Supination.

fig 8 fig 9

While this 'magical move' freaks out the newly converted; the longer you can 'flow the left wrist' into this bowed position the better (all the way to the ½ or even the ¾ follow through position). Eventually, with practice, the results are absolutely astounding. *Don't be afraid to exaggerate this move.*

This movement was previously discussed in lesson 2 (Contact). If the hands are leading the club-head through the hitting area, Supination will be achieved (figure 8). Bowing the left wrist toward the target will contribute strongly to that all-important divot, which is taken after the ball (refer to page 35, fig 4)

Eventually Contact Supination and Directional Supination will need to be combined to create one fluid movement. When this left handed action becomes a comfortable part of the swing, a player has tremendous potential to excel.

When done correctly, this two-fold movement should produce a low hook, indicating a healthy and workable foundation to build on.

Negative Pronation

Also known as scooping, left hand pronation through impact (figure 11) is the opposite of the correct supinating action. When the club head passes the hands, the 'cupped' or scooped left wrist will be facing up making it impossible to hit the ball solid because the club will be on its way up rather than down through impact (fig 9).

fig 10 fig 11

During the swing motion, left hand pronation is needed in the backswing and downswing only. It is not until impact that the left hand will make the transition to supination (refer to figure 7).

If the left hand continues to pronate through impact (figure 10), power will be lost and a multitude of errors can take place – particularly the dreaded shank.

The Shanks

With the exception of slicing, *shanking* (hitting a golf ball with the 'heel area' of an iron club) is without a doubt the most common and most frustrating error for the inexperienced player to overcome, simply because they are often not able to detect it. The heel area is where the shaft meets the blade of an iron, thus forming 'a corner'. It can be a very confusing part of the club. Shanking is so common and the heel area so confusing I have often wondered why the manufacturers haven`t done something about it. Possibly having the shaft and head built with different metals so when the 'heel area' was hit, it would make a loud and definite sound. This would be a huge help for the learning player because they wouldn`t be able to assume, as so many do, that they had topped the ball. Shanking is much more common than topping. This particular shot problem is even feared by many instructors, thinking it`s an incurable disease and they might catch it. There are many who are even afraid to say the word shank, referring to it as the dreaded-S or the Sherman Tank. If I were afraid to talk about or watch a person shanking I would not have a job, because eight out of every ten students I start teaching in a season have the Shanks and don`t even know it!

The confusion with Shanking is that there are 3 different negative shot patterns that can occur. The ball can go right, left, or straight along the ground. A shanked ball can go anywhere, often being hard to detect. The only common characteristic to this shot is no matter how it`s hit it's always ugly.

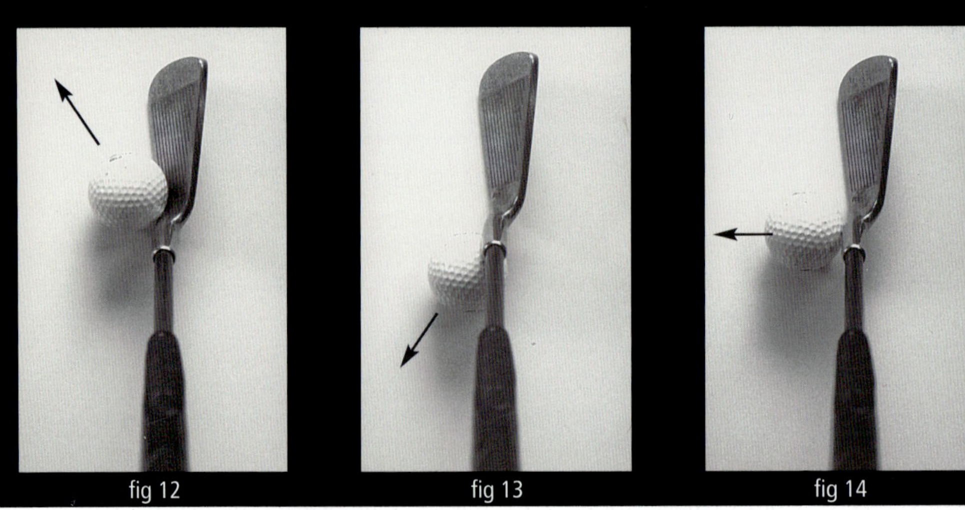

fig 12 fig 13 fig 14

The detection factor when evaluating your performance is extremely important. If your ball is not going up into the air as everyone desires, don't automatically assume you are topping it, the chances are much greater that you are shanking! Just to show you how difficult this part of the club is to evaluate, here is an example of a man I was teaching one day. His name was Paul and he had been playing golf for about ten years, he was thirty-five years old and appeared to be quite a good player. I had Paul start our lesson by hitting a few seven irons to loosen up while we got acquainted. As he was hitting balls I noticed that he had a good golf swing. It was technically very sound, but every shot was a shank that travelled to the right (figure 12). I watched about fifteen shots then asked Paul, "how can I help you today?", to which he answered that he was desperate to get rid of the shanks. Apparently he had been experiencing this problem for about two months. I continued to watch him hit balls for a few minutes and found myself amazed at the consistency of his shank; without exception every single shot hit the inside corner of the club. After every shank-shot he would say, "I`m shanking it, aren`t I?" I would reply, "yes you sure are." As I continued to watch in total amazement, I was trying to figure out exactly what I could do to help this poor guy. Finally I decided after some deliberation to have him confirm the location of the strike. I held his club in the air and had him point to where he thought the shank area was located. To my amazement, Paul pointed to the toe of his club – I was shocked! I informed him that where he was pointing was not the shank, it was the toe! He was hitting every ball off the heel and thought he was hitting off the toe; a huge detection error! And he was an eight handicap! You can well imagine how he felt. After we had a good laugh together Paul resumed hitting balls and to no surprise, his shanks were gone. Since then I have found many individuals similar to Paul, but usually golfers who experience the shanks think they are *topping* the ball.

All shankers share one thing in common; they pronate through impact (figure 10), the opposite of the correct supinating action as discussed earlier in this lesson. This common problem, also known as scooping is almost always self induced, stemming from the inability to find the location of the strike. A typical example; a player shanks five shots in a row. Because the ball isn`t getting up into the air, the player says, "I`m just not getting under it!" Mistakenly, the player will start to scoop (pronate) through the hitting area, trying to 'get under it', thus regressing further from the desired supinating action.

In closing lesson 4, it is important to understand that during your development shanking might happen from time to time, as will fat and thin shots – this is normal and to be expected. Until coordination is built up through repetition, expect anything, but keep moving forward. Avoid Pronation (scooping) through the hitting area. This movement is shared by more than 85% of golfers according to my calculations, and can be disastrous to your long term progress. The pronating golfer doesn`t have much chance to excel at golf because he is more vulnerable to errors such as; Shanking, Fat shots, Thin shots and Slicing, not to mention a complete loss of power. Supination through impact is an essential component of the standard swing; as the famous Ben Hogan would say "it is a must!" Pronation does have its place in specialty shots that are used in about 1% of the shots you will ever make. You would be well advised to focus on the other 99% instead.

Practice With a Purpose

Do you love practicing, I sure do! I have always enjoyed finding places to practice within a big city like Vancouver. I love discovering that cool spot where I can take my shag balls, whether its the beach, the airport, or any open space where I am all alone to do what I love to do – hit balls! I try to tell this to my students all the time; "Get yourself a bag of balls, go here, go there, search for turf. It`s great for your game and it`s free!" You don`t have to be at a golf course to practice, you just need a bag of practice balls.

So you have your own practice balls now, and you`ve found a place to hit them, great! So what`s the goal? I`ll always remember this quote from my junior days,:"He hit a bag of seven irons and you could have thrown a blanket over them." Exaggerated perhaps, but a tight spread is the goal. Let`s say your practice bag has fifty balls in it, and you`re going to hit them all with a nine iron, your goal would be to have all fifty balls end up very close together. If you find that your spread is quite erratic and your balls are flying all over the place, then you`re trying to hit them too far. Don`t start too big, start small: 60 yards, then 100 yards, etc. How tight is your spread? Show control.

Practicing at a driving range is not the best environment for improving your game, even though it can be convenient. You can usually park your car very close, you don`t have to pick up any balls, and you can practice under cover when it`s raining or, at night, under the lights. These are the positives and they have a lot of merit, especially in today`s high paced lifestyle. The negatives, however, present a challenge for your improvement. For example, at a driving range, you are not able to see your 'spread'. Even the word DRIVING range instills power. Use the driver, hit it as far and as crooked as you can. Control? Who needs control? Somebody else picks them up. When it comes to comparing mats versus turf or sand: because of the high cost of maintaining the turf at a driving range, it has become increasingly rare to find a range with grass to hit off. Mats are the norm, especially in colder climates. We practice off a mat yet we play off grass, talk about different! Hitting off a mat cannot provide you with the all important divot pattern. Mats also instill a false sense of security because the clubhead bounces into the ball when you hit it 'fat' allowing you to believe that your contact is great until you get out to play. Hitting off grass or sand will not build false illusions into your game. Also, because of the wood or cement base that is underneath the mat, you can hurt yourself through repeated impact– I did.

Practice with a purpose – hopefully this doesn`t sound too regimented. This is not meant to imply that you can`t have fun, just be aware that the purpose of practice is to build consistency. The concepts put forth in Smash and Carve are there for that very reason. But this can only happen if you practice with some regularity. The more you practice the luckier you`ll get. If you don`t practice, who knows? It will be a guessing game from day to day. There will never be a replacement for hard work, which makes me laugh a little when I think about golf club technology. This driver hits it further, this club spins more, this putter sinks more; it`s all fine equipment but it will never provide you with a truly sound game. Manufacturers have gotten to the point where they are going backwards. Now the popular slogan is, 'oversize is over-rated!' This, after most players own oversize drivers. Where does it end? The simple truth is, a good player can play well with anything, it doesn't matter much what they use because, "it`s not the tool, it`s the fool behind the tool". It is important to have a decent set of clubs, but after that it`s all developed talent; 98% individual, 2% equipment. You can`t buy a game, you have to earn it.

There are many different ways to approach the game given that both physical and mental aspects are almost always involved. The less experienced a player is, the more physical the game is — for a beginner, it`s 90% physical. There is a popular saying that 'golf is 90% mental'. If this is so, why do we have to practice all the physical stuff? This saying likely applies only to the expert player, yet ironically these are the game's best players *and they practice the most*! Their considerable investment of time and effort to building and fine-tuning physical skills would suggest a more intimate connection between skill competence and mental confidence — building confidence through consistency and consistency through confidence.

A regular practice routine will develop consistent muscle memory. Throughout these lessons we have been developing your knowledge base and your physical skills for golf. It`s important to realize that these skills will be practiced over the long term, and improvement may be slow, but slow will be relative. How many balls are you willing to hit a week? If you hit 200 - 500 balls a week and play twice a week your improvement will be continuous. If you hit 50 balls once in a while and play semi-monthly, improvement will be minimal. Golf is a numbers game where regular practice is rewarded with results.

The purpose behind Smash & Carve is to provide you, the developing golfer, with the correct terminology, the key elements of movement, and a direct approach to learning and understanding the nuts and bolts of the golf swing. Smash & Carve provides a sure, steady foundation to build on with any good teaching professional. For now, you are able to communicate the language of the game and are armed with the understanding of contact and direction. Dedicating yourself today to a positive training program will help to encourage your steady progress as you continue to discover and enjoy the art of ball striking.